Legally Driving the 50 States of the USA

California

All the information you need to make your California car trip safe & hassle free!

TOLL ROADS AND RATES

The toll roads in CA are paid for by cash, or if you are a resident subscriber with FasTrak™, which you pay for monthly through your credit card. The tolls start at .25¢ and increases to $10 (one way) dependent on the peak hours and flow of traffic using the toll roads. The more cars on the toll road, the more they will charge. Trucks can cost up to $20.00 one way. Make sure to keep change and cash handy when using toll roads.

SAN JOAQUIN HILLS (73) TOLL ROAD NEW TOLL RATES EFFECTIVE JULY 2, 2007

Peak = Monday-Friday, Northbound 7-9 a.m. & Southbound 4-7 p.m.
Off-peak = All other weekday hours and holidays
Locations:

Aliso Creek Road	El Toro/Laguna Canyon Road
Bonita Canyon	La Paz Road/Moulton Parkway
Catalina View Mainline	Newport Coast

FOOTHILL/EASTERN (241, 261, 133) TOLL RATES NEW TOLL RATES EFFECTIVE JULY 2, 2007

Peak = Monday-Friday, Northbound 7-9 a.m. & Southbound 4-7 p.m.;
*At this location, Peak = Monday-Friday, Southbound 7-9 a.m. & Northbound 4-7 p.m.
Off-peak = All other weekday hours and holidays
Locations:

Antonio Parkway	Orange Grove Mainline
Irvine Boulevard East	Portola Parkway North
Irvine Boulevard West	Portola Parkway South
*Irvine Ranch Mainline	Portola Parkway West
Los Alisos Parkway	Tomato Springs Mainline
Windy Ridge Mainline	

FasTrak™ is a private company-owned electronic toll-system used on the toll ways in California allowing drivers to drive through "FasTrak™ Only" lanes without stopping. The toll is automatically deducted from a prepaid account.

You can also pay tolls with cash on the 73, 241, 133 and 261 Toll Roads™. However, some toll booths are not staffed and you will need the exact change or cash at the automatic coin machines.

(Note: Cash is not accepted on the 91 Express Lanes, which is run by a separate entity from The Toll Roads™. To order a transponder for use on the 91 Express Lanes, call 1-800-600-9191.)

TRAFFIC CONDITIONS & REPORTS

Northern CA/Bay Area

KCBS (AM 740) in the Bay Area, every ten minutes, 24/7
KQED FM (88.5) every 10 to 15 minutes during rush hours.
Satellite Radio 24/7 with navigation system, subscriber only

Los Angeles County

KCBS (740AM) every 10 minutes
KFWB News (980 AM) every 10 minutes
Satellite Radio 24/7 with navigation system, subscriber only

San Diego Area

KCBQ (1170 AM) during news
KOGO (600 AM) during news
Satellite Radio 24/7 with navigation system, subscriber only

Call Caltrans 800-427-7623 for information of road conditions in the state.

SPEED LIMITS

The most important speed limits you need to know are the two "standard" limits of 35 MPH and 55 MPH.

- Residential Streets and School crossing: 25 MPH (40 KPM)
- Commercial Streets 35 MPH (56 KPM)
- Freeways and Highways 55 to 65 MPH (88-105 KPM)

READ THE SPEED SIGNS AND FOLLOW THE FLOW OF TRAFFIC.

When the freeways are congested you'll find yourself driving at 10-20 MPH. Give yourself time.

CELL PHONE LAWS

CA Wireless Tele Act, effective July 1, 2008, prohibits drivers from operating their vehicles using a hand-held phone. Hands-free devices are acceptable for adults only. If you are under 18 years of age, you are not allowed to use cell phones and/or any communication devices while driving.

First offense $20, and $50 per offense thereafter.

NO SMOKING CITIES AND BEACHES

These beaches and piers do not allow smoking:

Huntington Beach, Laguna Beach, Long Beach, Los Angeles, Malibu, Newport Beach, San Clemente, Santa Monica, Seal Beach, Solana Beach

These cities are currently thinking of banning smoking in parks:

- Hermosa Beach (Considering smoke free beaches)
- Redondo Beach (Considering smoke free beaches)
- Santa Ana (Considering smoke free parks)

The following cities in California have smoking bans in parks and recreational areas:

- Beverly Hills (in parks)
- El Cajon (in parks and recreational areas)
- El Monte (in playgrounds and Tot Lots)
- La Puente (in public places)
- Long Beach (in playgrounds and Tot Lots)
- Pasadena (in parks including Golf Course)
- San Fernando (in parks and recreation centers)
- Santa Cruz (Beach Boardwalk is a non-smoking facility considering extending ban to beaches)
- Santa Monica (in parks)
- Seal Beach (on pier)

CAR KEY REPLACEMENTS

If you need a copy of your car key, it won't be easy if you drive a car that requires copies from a dealer only. If you drive one of the cars below, make sure you don't need an e

Locksmiths will not re

mobiles:

Audi	
Jaguar	
Mazda	Mercedes-Benz
Mini	Porsche
Saab	Volkswagen
Volvo	

May be a little tough to get a copy, but it can be done:

Buick	Cadillac
Chevrolet	Chrysler
Dodge	GMC
Jeep	Lexus
Oldsmobile	Plymouth
Pontiac	Scion
Toyota	

All other auto keys can be easily copied.

PARKING RULES FOR SAN FRANCISCO AND LOS ANGELES

SAN FRANCISCO Suggestion—take public transportation and taxis if you are staying in the city, you'll get around a lot faster and cheaper. But, if you must drive then be aware of the difficulty and cost of parking. Park on a residential street and then walk, the blocks aren't long and there is a lot to look at, especially in commercial areas like Union Square and Fisherman's Wharf.

- If you park on the street, make sure you don't park in the red (not even an inch).
- Don't park past the slope of a driveway.
- Don't park in a Red Zone.
- Don't park in a Yellow Zone, only for commercial vehicles.
- Don't park in a Green Zone (10 minute limit) and White Zones (5 minute limit).
- Don't park within 15 feet of a Fire Hydrant.
- You can park at a broken meter, but the time limit still applies.

LOS ANGELES The difference with LA and SF is that SF has a very good public transportation system and LA does not. LA's public transportation, better than ten years ago, but still lacking in terms of areas covered and the time it takes to get to your destination. It may be worth it to park on a residential street and walk, because the restaurants and clubs take over all parking in front of their venues at night. Bottom line--you do need a car in Los Angeles.

- Don't park on a Yellow Zone from 7am to 6pm, Monday-Saturday, and not at all on Sunday.
- Don't park on a Green Zone from 8am to 6pm, Monday-Saturday.
- Don't park on a "permit only" street unless you have a permit. The tickets are steep.
- When parking at a meter, make sure to note whether the end time is 6pm (the usual) or 10pm (the greedy).
- There are parking garages in Westwood and Beverly Hills where you can park from 1-2 hours for free, look for them.
- Parking meters in some cities will accept credit cards, meter keys, and/or coins.

ALL INFORMATION ABOUT PARKING IS SUPERCEDED BY THE PARKING SIGNS—READ THEM AND FOLLOW INSTRUCTIONS TO AVOID TICKETS OR HAVING YOUR CAR TOWED.

TICKETS RANGE FROM $35-$45. And....if a meter person is around, put money in the meter regardless if there is still time on it, otherwise you can be ticketed for "stealing" meter time.

DRINKING AND DRIVING

Estimated Costs for a First Misdemeanor DUI

The following list is applied to a first misdemeanor DUI offense in California and can cost you (or your parents) up to $11,000, and subsequent DUI offenses carry much harsher penalties:

- Fines
- Penalty Assessment
- Tow/Impound Fee
- Alcohol Education classes (3-12 months)
- Car insurance dropped and/or cost increase
- State Restitution Fund
- DMV License Re-issue fee
- Attorney and legal fees

Not included above, but will cost you: lost wages from work time, medical costs for the injured parties if the cost is beyond your insurance medical limit, the car's property damage, and then if you're privately sued by someone injured in the accident.

Don't drink and drive.

CALIFORNIA LAW: Parents and others providing the alcohol can be held criminally liable for contributing to the delinquency of a minor. Parents have been found guilty of contributing to the delinquency of a minor when they have encouraged minors to drink. A parent may not be liable for injuries to the minor or others involved, but adults convicted of giving alcohol to a minor are guilty of a misdemeanor, and must pay a fine of $1,000 and do a minimum of 24 hours of community service. Moreover, if the minor gets in an accident and causes great bodily injury to himself or others, the adult faces a jail sentence of six months to one year, as well as a fine of up to $1,000. (B&PC §§ 25602.1, 25658)

(SB 1756)--Increases the mandatory suspension of driver licenses from 6 months to 10 months for any first DUI offense when the person's blood alcohol content (BAC) is .20 or higher. The legal threshold for a DUI offense is .08.

CAR INSURANCE REQUIREMENTS

Minimum Liability:

- $15,000 for injury/death to one person.
- $30,000 for injury/death to more than one person.
- $5,000 for damage to property.

(CA Insurance Code §11580.1b)

REMEMBER—YOU ARE NOT THE ONLY ONE ON THE ROAD

1. Use your turn signals, other drivers cannot read your mind and they will not be able to react properly to your driving.

2. To drive in California, you need patience to avoid road rage. We're all in it together, so take a deep breath and stay calm. And don't forget to stop at red lights and stop signs!

FREEWAY SERVICE PATROL

The Freeway Service Patrol (FSP) is a joint program provided by Caltrans, the California Highway Patrol (CHP) and the local transportation agency. The FSP provides service to motorists at no cost.

You can dial #399 from your cell phone in order to obtain roadside assistance

If you get stuck on the freeway because your automobile stops running, FSP can help. For example, FSP will:

- Offer you a gallon of gas, if you run out.
- "Jump start" your car if the battery is dead.
- Refill your radiator and tape hoses.
- Even change a flat tire.

Note: The FSP program...

- Cannot tow your vehicle to a private repair service or residence.
- Does not recommend tow service companies, repair or body shops.
- Does not tow motorcycles.
- Does not assist vehicles which have been involved in accidents, unless directed by CHP.
- Does report any accident to the CHP.

If FSP cannot get your car going, it will be towed free of charge to a location approved by the CHP. FSP will also contact additional assistance for you. The CHP will notify an auto club or towing service.

The FSP serves the following areas:

- Border Division - the San Diego and Orange County areas
- Central Division - the Fresno area
- Coastal Division - the Monterey and Santa Cruz areas
- Golden Gate Division - the San Francisco Bay area
- Inland Division - the Riverside area
- Southern Division - the Los Angeles area
- Valley Division - the Sacramento Metro and Tracy areas

FIRE, ACCIDENT, HIGHWAY DEBRIS (couch, paint, etc.) — Call CHP (CA Highway Patrol or 911)

AUTO CLUB OF AMERICA: 1-800-400-4222
DRIVER AMERICA AUTO CLUB: 1-866-494-6402

CALIFORNIA FREEWAY TRIVIA:

*Los Angeles has the busiest freeway system in the nation with 27 Interstate freeways, 17 Highways, 231 Freeways, and 6 county routes. *The San Francisco Bay Area has the 2nd busiest overall freeway system in the nation, and is the most congested in terms of percentage of congested miles, hours of delay and average speeds. *Sacramento has one of the busiest freeway systems in the country, and the busiest in the world for a population of under 3 million. *LA drivers lose 72 hours a year, and San Diego 57 hours due to congested freeways and highways.

Automotive/Travel/Informational USA $9.95 Canada $12.95

WHAT TO DO IF YOUR CAR BREAKS DOWN

- If your car breaks down, DON'T LEAVE IT. Use your cell phone to call for help.
- If you don't see a call box within eye distance or remember passing by one, then forget it, and stay with your car.
- If you do not have a cell phone or even if you do, then periodically while on a road trip contact one or two people (one at destination and one at the departure point) and update them along your trip so, if they don't hear from you, then they know to look for you.

ALWAYS CARRY IN YOUR CAR

In a carryall bag or backpack (for easy transfer if you rent a car):

- A set of jumper cables
- A first aid kit
- A solid flashlight with extra batteries
- Glass cleaner & paper towels
- Even if you have a GPS, still have some maps in your car.
- To stay awake, use Audio books, CDs, and especially satellite radio if you drive long distances on a regular basis.
- Water (for yourself and for your car's radiator, if you plan to drive in high heat)
- Cell phone battery device (like Energizer ™ or Cellboost™) made for charging your cell phone just in case your car battery dies
- Gaffer's or Duct tape in bright yellow to mark the hood of your car with an SOS sign if you become stranded
- Blankets in the trunk
- Always keep a small overnight bag with a jacket, socks, sneakers, etc, just in case you are stranded and you need to switch from sandals to shoes. This is good to have if there is a fire, an earthquake, or just lost and stuck in your car overnight.
- If you wear glasses, use them, and use sunglasses when in very sunny areas for the strong glare.
- DO NOT – put people in the trunk of your car (even for a short distance), it's against the law as well as dangerous.

DRIVING IN CERTAIN WEATHER CONDITIONS

FOG—There are certain areas where fog is especially thick and difficult to drive through. Use your AMBER lights, not your bright or regular headlights; slow down your speed because you lose sight of any landmarks and you will drive faster without you realizing it. The AMBER lights are more easily seen through the fog according to some car manufacturers.

EXTREME HEAT—Make sure your car's radiator is in good condition if you plan to drive through the desert, and take a lot of water. Turn off your air conditioner (I know… but the heat!) when you drive on steep inclines, the harder your car has to work, then the less you want to stress your car. If it's three digit heat in the desert, don't drive unless you have to.

RAIN—Slow Down! Everyone drives in CA as though driving in the rain and dry weather is the same, and it's not. Be sure your window wipers are in good condition and use your headlights. If you see steep flooding, don't check it out to make sure it's not too steep. Turn around and take another route so your car doesn't end up on the news with you being lifted by helicopter (which you have to pay for by the way).

WEBSITES TO VISIT

www.drivingtheusa.com

www.fuelcostcalculator.com (Calculate how much it will cost to drive from point A to point B dependent on your vehicle model and year.)
www.thetollroads.com/home/index.htm (Calculate how much the toll roads will cost you if you use them.)
www.parkingspacenow.smgov.net (Shows you up-to-the-minute availability of parking spaces in the City of Santa Monica parking lots.)

ISBN: 978-0-9800246-0-9
50995
9 780980 024609